# Hey Beautiful!

Author: Tanya Hall

# Hey Beautiful!

Go with me for a minute in your imagination. Come on in and have a seat on my sofa. I've written this workbook for women like us—to remind us that even when we stumble, we don't have to fall.

Life leaves marks! I've come to realize that we are all in some stage of healing and recovery, and we will be until the day we finally get to heaven. This 7-week heart checkup—like a spring cleaning or a fresh start—is your opportunity to notice when old patterns begin creeping back in, to grow deeper in Christ in the areas where you're already strong, and to find new freedom where He wants to bring healing.

Each week you'll find:

- Tanya's Story. A short video where I share a personal story to set the stage

- Five days of guided activities. Each week includes Scripture, old mindsets, new mind shifts, an activity, reflection, and writing prompts including writing a statement of declaration, prayer, and sometimes space to write your own prayer

- A Hey Beautiful Sister Session.. A group video where women discuss the lessons after walking through them together

- Sister Share questions you can use if you're doing this workbook with a group

- A daily reflection space to record your thoughts, feelings, and insights

- A memory verse card to carry with you throughout the week


This book is a beautiful journey you can revisit again and again. Your time with the Lord will walk you through some of the common struggles we all face, offering a new perspective and fresh grace.

I want you to know that I am praying for you. May God use these pages to remind you just how loved, chosen, and treasured you are.

Completely His,

Tanya Hall

# Acknowledgments

First, thank you to First Lady Marilyn Brown for recognizing the power in the simple words "Hey Beautiful." You were the one who spoke life over this phrase and saw what I couldn't yet see. As I was preparing to write this book, you said, "That's the name of your book. It's a logo. It's what you say all the time." Thank you for doing what you do best, naming people, speaking life, and seeing the God-given identity in others. It's truly a gift, and I'm grateful that you used it to help me find the name for this work.

To my best friend, Samantha Hubarth, thank you for not only cheering me on as I take on new challenges but also for editing this book with such love and patience. I'm beyond thankful that you still love me after that process! Your support means the world to me.

To my amazing husband, Dion, thank you for continuously encouraging me to become everything God created me to be. Thank you for not only saying that with your words, but for showing it through your actions, making space for me to write, create, and breathe this vision into life. And thank you for tackling the tedious work of formatting to make sure every detail fit just right. Including all the editing of our videos. I'm so grateful to have you by my side. I love you! WE forever.

And lastly, but above all, thank you to God—my Rescuer, my Healer, my Best Friend, and my Creator. You never give up on me. You fill me with purpose, peace, and creativity. Every word I write is a reflection of Your grace.

Forever and always—completely Yours.

Tanya Hall

# Table of Contents

| | |
|---|---|
| Lesson One: Loved Already | 10 |
| Lesson Two: There is Only ONE You | 16 |
| Lesson Three: When People Pleasing Becomes a Prison | 24 |
| Lesson Four: What If I Loved Me Too? | 32 |
| Lesson Five: Taking Down Strongholds- Lies Are No Longer Protected | 40 |
| Lesson Six: Believing the Truth Over How You Feel | 52 |
| Week Seven: Sit, Surrender, and Soar | 62 |
| Closing Reflections | 72 |
| Memory Verse Cards | 74 |

## Lesson One:

# Loved Already

# Lesson One: Loved Already

## Day 1

**Key Verse to Memorize:**

Romans 5:8 (NIV) "But God demonstrates his own love for us in this: While we were still sinners, Christ died for us."

**Tanya's Story.** Scan the QR code.

Hey Beautiful! Video Lesson One

**Reflection + Writing Prompts:** When I first fell in love with Jesus, it felt like…

**Mind Shift Moment:**

Old Mindset: God loves me more when I do more.

New Mind Shift: Even on my worst day, Christ said I was worth dying for.

**The Blessing:** May you no longer work to prove your worth but know your worth.

**Prayer:** Lord Jesus, thank You for loving me so much and unconditionally. Thank You for being the WAY for me to have a relationship with God. I want to be transformed more and more into Your likeness, and I want desperately to believe that Your Love is steadfast. I give You all of me anew today. In Jesus' Name, Amen.

# Lesson One: Loved Already

## Day 2

---

**Key Verse to Memorize:**

Romans 5:8 (NIV) "But God demonstrates his own love for us in this: While we were still sinners, Christ died for us."

**Message:**

Before you chose God, He chose you. Before you cleaned yourself up, He called you worthy. Before you got your act together, He died for you. God's love isn't based on your performance, your pain, or your past. It's not affected by your worst decisions or your best behavior. It's constant. It's undeserved. It's steadfast. This is not about salvation; that's your decision to follow Christ. But His love for you? That was His decision. And He decided you were worth dying for.

You don't have to earn love that's already been given. Even on your worst day, God says you're worth dying for.

**Fill in the Blank Section:** Romans 5:8 (NIV)

But God _____ his own love for us in this: While we were still _____, Christ _____ for us.

**Reflection + Writing Prompts:** What makes it hard to truly believe that even on my worst day, I'm worth dying for?

**Mind Shift Moment:**

Old Mindset: God loves me more when I do more.

New Mind Shift: Even on my worst day, Christ said I was worth dying for.

**Prayer:** Lord Jesus, thank You, thank You for showing Your love for me even in the midst of my sin! That's so hard for my mind to accept. Your love is so perfect! Lord, please transform my mind. I want to see things like You do, including how You see me.. In Jesus' name, Amen.

# Lesson One: Loved Already

## Day 3

---

**Key Verse to Memorize:**

Romans 5:8 (NIV) "But God demonstrates his own love for us in this: While we were still sinners, Christ died for us."

**Sister Share Time:**

Grab a cup of coffee and join us for today's **Hey Beautiful Sister Session**– real women, honest conversation. Scan the QR code.

Sister Share Week One

- What part of this lesson spoke to you the most?
- Do certain experiences make it hard for you to receive love, especially God's love?
- Share one place in your life where God's love is starting to feel more real.

**Mind Shift Moment:**

Old Mindset: God loves me more when I do more.

New Mind Shift: Even on my worst day, Christ said I was worth dying for.

**Song of the Week:** "My Life Is in Your Hands" by Kathy Troccoli and Kirk Franklin version

**Prayer:** Lord, help me walk today as someone who is already loved… continue with your own personal prayer.

# Lesson One: Loved Already

## Day 4

---

**Key Verse to Memorize:**

Romans 5:8 (NIV) "But God demonstrates his own love for us in this: While we were still sinners, Christ died for us."


**Activity:**

Find a mirror. Look into it. Say these words out loud: "Even on my worst day, Christ thought I was worth dying for."

Write what it felt like to say it: _____

If you're brave enough, text someone else and say: Hey, Beautiful, just a reminder: Even on your worst day, Christ thought you were worth dying for.


**Mind Shift Moment:**

Old Mindset: God loves me more when I do more.

New Mind Shift: Even on my worst day, Christ said I was worth dying for.


**Dig Deeper:** Read Luke 15: the parable of the lost sheep, the lost coin, and the prodigal son.


**The Blessing:** May you begin to love yourself like God does.


**Prayer:** Lord of my life, the One who knows me and chose me, and my sweet Lord, You keep choosing me. Lord Jesus, I ask You to keep the truth of Your love as my very foundation. Make it so strong. And help me to love like You. In Jesus' name, Amen.

# Lesson One: Loved Already

## Day 5

---

**Key Verse to Memorize:**

Romans 5:8 (NIV) "But God demonstrates his own love for us in this: While we were still sinners, Christ died for us."

**Declaration Statement:**

I declare_____

**Reflection + Writing Prompts:** This is a transformative moment, a mind-shifting moment, when you see your worth as God sees your worth. What truth is God wanting to write on your heart?

**Mind Shift Moment:**

Old Mindset: God loves me more when I do more.

New Mind Shift: Even on my worst day, Christ said I was worth dying for.

**The Blessing:** May you apply all the scriptures of love and adoration for God's people to yourself, too.

**Prayer:** Lord, knowing that you love me unconditionally, makes me want to serve You and please you even more. Abiding in your love holds me steady. I worship You. I give myself to You anew. Thank You. In Jesus' Name. Amen

## Lesson Two:

# There is Only ONE You

# Lesson Two: There is Only ONE You

## Day 1

---

**Key Verse to Memorize:**

Galatians 6:4 (NIV) "Each one should test their own actions. Then they can take pride in themselves alone, without comparing themselves to someone else,"

**Tanya's Story.** Scan the QR code.

Hey Beautiful! Video Lesson Two

**Reflection + Writing Prompts:** Ask the Holy Spirit to highlight your own gifts, interests, and even things you dislike. What did He reveal to you?

**Mind Shift Moment:**

Old Mindset: I need to be like them to succeed.

New Mind Shift: There is only ONE me, and God made me on purpose.

**The Blessing:**

And may your heart rest in this truth: There is only ONE you—and God calls you very good.

**Prayer:** Lord Jesus, seal these truths in our minds so that we may see, think, and live representing You more and more in our own unique way. In Jesus' name. Amen.

# Lesson Two: There is Only ONE You

## Day 2

---

**Key Verse to Memorize:**

Galatians 6:4 (NIV) "Each one should test their own actions. Then they can take pride in themselves alone, without comparing themselves to someone else,"

**Message:**

1 Corinthians 7:17 (NIV) "Nevertheless, each person should live as a believer in whatever situation the Lord has assigned to them, just as God has called them. This is the rule I lay down in all the churches."

Each of us should live the life the Lord has assigned to us, our gifts, our temperament, our story — they're not an accident.

Read 1 Samuel 17:39-40.

David, just a boy, was willing to fight Goliath. Saul tried to give David his armor, but it didn't fit. Saul was a head taller than everyone else, and David was just a boy! David couldn't even walk in it. Trying to wear someone else's armor caused David to stumble! And it does the same to us.

When we try to live someone else's calling or admire someone else's gifts so much that we try to be them, we stumble.

God has given YOU armor to wear. Use your own gear. Walk in your own calling. And let's not pressure others to fit into our armor either. This world needs all kinds - different voices, skills, temperaments, and perspectives.

You are uniquely equipped for the room you're in. Nobody else can fill your spot.

**Fill in the Blank Section:** Galatians 6:4 (NIV)

Each one should _____ their own _____. Then they can take _____ in themselves alone, without _____ themselves to someone else,

- Write this verse in your own words.
- What part of it jumps out at you today? _____

**Reflection + Writing Prompts:** What's one unique trait about you that shows His glory? Who is it that you sometimes try to be like?

**Mind Shift Moment:**

Old Mindset: I need to be like them to succeed.

New Mind Shift: There is only ONE me, and God made me on purpose.

**Prayer:** Lord, as I see my own strengths and special qualities that You gave me, give me eyes to see unique gifts in others. Show me how You use each of our strengths and character traits to give a more complete picture of who You are to the world around us. May I always remember that in my own strength I can do nothing. It is only when I stay connected to You that I can be transformed into Your likeness. In Jesus' name. Amen

# Lesson Two: There is Only ONE You

## Day 3

**Key Verse to Memorize:**

Galatians 6:4 (NIV) "Each one should test their own actions. Then they can take pride in themselves alone, without comparing themselves to someone else,"

**Sister Share Time:**

Grab a cup of coffee and join us for today's **Hey Beautiful Sister Session**– real women, honest conversation. Scan the QR code.

Sister Share Week Two

- 💬 Share one way you've tried to wear someone else's armor.
- 💬 Talk about one unique quality you're learning to love in yourself.
- 💬 Encourage each other to walk confidently in your own gear.

**Mind Shift Moment:**

Old Mindset: I need to be like them to succeed.

New Mind Shift: There is only ONE me, and God made me on purpose.

**Song of the Week:** "Free to Be Me", by Francesca Battistelli. Let this song remind you that you are free to be you, dents and all.

**Prayer:** Lord, I want to be free to be the me that you uniquely created me to be, without comparing myself to others. Please help me see myself... continue with your own personal prayer.

# Lesson Two: There is Only ONE You

## Day 4

**Key Verse to Memorize:**

Galatians 6:4 (NIV) "Each one should test their own actions. Then they can take pride in themselves alone, without comparing themselves to someone else,"

**Activity:**

Take yourself on a 'dream shopping' date. Go alone. Visit stores you wouldn't normally enter.

Pay attention:

- What colors catch your eye?
- What things make you smile?
- What do you find yourself drawn to?

This is a way to get to know the you God created—and delight in it!

If you want, take a picture of one thing that inspired you and write a few words about it.

**Mind Shift Moment:**

Old Mindset: I need to be like them to succeed.

New Mind Shift: There is only ONE me, and God made me on purpose.

**Dig Deeper:** Read 1 Corinthians 12:14-18

**The Blessing:** May your confidence grow in who God made you to be.

**Prayer:** Lord, thank You for making me uniquely me. Please show me the special qualities in me that represent You. Give me eyes to see me the way that You see me. In Jesus' name, Amen.

# Lesson Two: There is Only ONE You

## Day 5

---

**Key Verse to Memorize:**

Galatians 6:4 (NIV) "Each one should test their own actions. Then they can take pride in themselves alone, without comparing themselves to someone else,"

**Reflection + Writing Prompts:** Let this be a transformative moment, a mind-shifting moment, when you see your worth as God sees your worth. What truth is God wanting to write on your heart?

**Mind Shift Moment:**

Old Mindset: I need to be like them to succeed.

New Mind Shift: There is only ONE me, and God made me on purpose.

**Declaration Statement:**

I declare_____

**The Blessing:** May you stop striving to wear what was never meant for you.

**Prayer:** Lord God, You are so patient with me. Thank You for loving me as I grow. Just like You planted the garden in Genesis and gave us the picture in John 15 that You are the Gardener, keep growing me. I know that You love to see me grow and are supplying all I need through the True Vine, Jesus Christ. Thank You, God. In Jesus' name, Amen.

## Lesson Three:

# When People Pleasing Becomes a Prison

# Lesson Three: When People Pleasing Becomes a Prison

## Day 1

**Key Verse to Memorize:**

Galatians 1:10 (NIV) "Am I now trying to win the approval of human beings, or of God? Or am I trying to please people? If I were still trying to please people, I would not be a servant of Christ."

**Tanya's Story**: Scan the QR code.

Hey Beautiful! Video Lesson Three

**Reflection + Writing Prompts:** Ask the Lord to give you sight to see if you are in a people-pleasing prison?

**Mind Shift Moment:**

Old Mindset: I need to make everyone happy.

New Mind Shift: I live for an audience of One.

**The Blessing:** May you become free in your serving.

**Prayer:** God, thank You so much for opening my eyes to the compromised priorities I've been walking in without even realizing. Thank You for giving me this time to be refreshed and renewed—to pause and make sure I'm still committed to the things You've already taught me, so I can keep walking in freedom. This week, show me any areas that need to be cleaned up or pruned—and please, be gentle with me. Thank You for loving me so tenderly and constantly. In Jesus' name. Amen.

# Lesson Three: When People Pleasing Becomes a Prison

# Day 2

**Key Verse to Memorize:**

Galatians 1:10 (NIV) "Am I now trying to win the approval of human beings, or of God? Or am I trying to please people? If I were still trying to please people, I would not be a servant of Christ."

**Message:**

People-pleasing can look a lot like kindness or selfless service. On the outside, it may even be praised. But underneath, if we're honest, it can quietly grow into something unhealthy. When our choices are controlled by the fear of disappointing others—or by the craving to be liked—we begin living out of pressure instead of purpose. Over time, we trade the truth of who we are for a performance that is exhausting, fragile, and fake.

God never asked you to carry the weight of keeping everyone happy. He never required you to earn your worth by being agreeable or constantly available. He never asked you to be everyone's favorite—He simply asks to be yours. His desire is for your heart, not your performance.

Idolatry is often described as lifting something or someone higher than God in our hearts. We may not carve statues or bow to golden calves, but when we give people's approval more influence than God's voice, we've elevated them to a place they were never meant to hold. Their opinions become our guide, and before we know it, we are worshiping at the altar of acceptance instead of walking in the freedom of grace.

But when we live for an audience of One, clarity begins to rise. We no longer scramble to keep everyone pleased. Instead, we learn to set boundaries—not as rebellion, but as reverence. We say "yes" or "no" with peace, not guilt, because our decisions are rooted in God's will. That kind of alignment brings freedom. It brings empowerment. And it helps us keep our priorities in order so that we stop betraying both ourselves and God.

**Fill in the Blank Section:** Galatians 1:10 (NIV)

Am I now trying to win the _____ of _____ beings, or of _____?

Or am I trying to _____ _____?

If I were still trying to _____ _____, I would not be a _____ of _____.

**Reflection + Writing Prompts:** Have you ever said no to the Holy Spirit and yes to a person, to make them happy?


**Mind Shift Moment:**

Old Mindset: I need to make everyone happy.

New Mind Shift: I live for an audience of One.


**Prayer:** Lord, thank You for teaching and teaching and teaching me again. Keep my heart soft as I listen to Your voice. I want to be free from pleasing people. Lord, forgive me for lifting other people's opinions of me higher than Yours. Keep speaking, Lord. I'm listening. In Jesus' name, Amen.

# Lesson Three: When People Pleasing Becomes a Prison

## Day 3

---

**Key Verse to Memorize:**

Galatians 1:10 (NIV) "Am I now trying to win the approval of human beings, or of God? Or am I trying to please people? If I were still trying to please people, I would not be a servant of Christ."

**Sister Share Time:**

Grab a cup of coffee and join us for today's **Hey Beautiful Sister Session**– real women, honest conversation. Scan the QR code.

Sister Share Week Three

💬 What affected you the most while reflecting on "not making people pleasing a prison?"

💬 What is one thing that you want to continue to implement in your daily life from this study?

💬 What did you learn about God and who He is this week so far?

**Mind Shift Moment:**

Old Mindset: I need to make everyone happy.

New Mind Shift: I live for an audience of One.

**Song of the Week:** "Audience of One", by Big Daddy Weave + "Only Jesus", by Casting Crowns

**Prayer:** Lord, set me free from trying to make _____ happy… continue with your own personal prayer.

# Lesson Three: When People Pleasing Becomes A Prison

## Day 4

**Key Verse to Memorize:**

Galatians 1:10 (NIV) "Am I now trying to win the approval of human beings, or of God? Or am I trying to please people? If I were still trying to please people, I would not be a servant of Christ."

**Activity:**

Take some quiet time with the Lord and ask Him to give you clarity about your priorities. Write them down in order—what comes first, second, and so on. Once you have your list, prayerfully consider:

How will you hold yourself accountable to live out these priorities daily?

Who could you invite to lovingly keep you accountable to the priorities God gives you?

Caution for married women: God designed marriage as a covenant, and in His order, your husband comes before your children. This doesn't diminish the love you give your children—it strengthens it. When your priorities reflect God's design, your family sees the fruit of peace and alignment. Pray over this truth and ask the Lord to help you live it out with grace.

**Mind Shift Moment:**

Old Mindset: I need to make everyone happy.

New Mind Shift: I live for an audience of One.

**Dig Deeper:** Read Colossians 3:23–24, Proverbs 29:25, and 1 Thessalonians 2:4

**The Blessing:** May you serve from the overflow of your heart….no longer serving to be filled.

**Prayer:** Lord, as I sit down to write out the priorities You've placed on my heart, lead me. Teach me to point others to the Savior, not try to be their savior. Give me ears that are attentive to Your voice. Help me this week to recognize where I need to make changes, and to celebrate the priorities You've already shifted in me, the ones I've held on to, and the victories I can already see. In Jesus' name. Amen.

# Lesson Three: When People Pleasing Becomes a Prison

## Day 5

---

**Key Verse to Memorize:**

Galatians 1:10 (NIV) "Am I now trying to win the approval of human beings, or of God? Or am I trying to please people? If I were still trying to please people, I would not be a servant of Christ."

**Declaration Statement:**

I declare_____

**Reflection + Writing Prompts:** Let this be a transformative moment, a mind-shifting moment, when you see your worth as God sees your worth. What truth is God wanting to write on your heart?

**Mind Shift Moment:**

Old Mindset: I need to make everyone happy.

New Mind Shift: I live for an audience of One.

**The Blessing:** May you be led by the Spirit as you say "yes" and "no" with a peaceful heart.

**Prayer:** Lord God, what freedom I've found in letting go of the weight of people-pleasing and the pressure to rescue others. Keep me here, Lord, in this free place of lifting your voice above all the other noise. Help me to make sure the people who are a priority in my life know it. Thank you for this time of growth and renewal. In Jesus' Name. Amen.

## Lesson Four:

# What If I Loved Me Too?

# Lesson Four: What If I Loved Me Too?

## Day 1

---

**Key Verses to Memorize:**

Matthew 22:37-39 (NIV) "Jesus replied, 'Love the Lord your God with all your heart and with all your soul and with all your mind.' This is the first and greatest commandment. And the second is like it: "Love your neighbor as yourself.""

Ephesians 2:8 (NIV) "For it is by grace you have been saved, through faith—and this is not from yourselves, it is the gift of God."

**Tanya's Story:** Scan the QR code.

Sister Share Week Four

**Reflection + Writing Prompts:** Where is it hard for you to give yourself grace?

**Mind Shift Moment:**

Old Mind Set: God loves me more when I'm perfect.

New Mind Shift: I am saved by grace, not by perfection.

**The Blessing:** May you live in the freedom of His grace purchased for you.

**Prayer:** Father, thank You that You don't require perfection. Thank You for loving me completely and seeing past all my striving. Help me forgive myself. Help me walk in the truth that grace is not just for the past, but for today. I don't want to live in shame or self-judgment. I want to be free. Teach me to love You with all my heart—and to love others as I learn to love myself. In Jesus' name. Amen.

# Lesson Four: What If I Loved Me Too?

## Day 2

**Key Verses to Memorize:**

Matthew 22:37-39 (NIV) "Jesus replied, 'Love the Lord your God with all your heart and with all your soul and with all your mind.' This is the first and greatest commandment. And the second is like it: "Love your neighbor as yourself."

Ephesians 2:8 (NIV) "For it is by grace you have been saved, through faith—and this is not from yourselves, it is the gift of God."

**Message:**

Last week, I messed up. Ten years later, I still got it wrong. But this time I didn't crawl into shame. I had the courage to ask God to search me and show me what was underneath. He answered. And I stayed in His love instead of running from it.

That's the power of grace. Not just grace for others. But grace for me, too.

God's love isn't earned; it's received. You were never expected to be perfect—just in His presence. Learning to love yourself is not selfish—it's obedience to what Jesus said. Grace is not only for your salvation; it's also for your healing, mistakes, growth, and your everyday journey.

In Galatians 5, Paul warns that if we try to earn salvation through our own works, then we're bound to keep the entire Law—a standard no one can meet. In that case, the cross loses its value to us.

Our actions are evidence that our faith is real, but they are not what save us. We are saved only through faith in Jesus—trusting in His finished work on the cross and His resurrection.

So, when we mess up, instead of staying stuck in the 'shame cycle', we can run to the Father's loving arms. There, we repent in His love—not running from it and not trying to earn it.

**Fill in the Blank Section:** Ephesians 2:8 (NIV)

For it is by _____ you have been _____, through _____ and this is not from _____, it is the _____ of _____.

**Reflection + Writing Prompts:** Is there something you need to forgive yourself for?

**Mind Shift Moment:**

Old Mind Set: God loves me more when I'm perfect.

New Mind Shift: I am saved by grace, not by perfection.

**Prayer:** God, My God, thank you for showing me my errors, my sins, my attitude. Forgive me. Please forgive me. You told us to forgive. Please help me, forgive myself, no more guilt, and no more shame. Only freedom in my game. In Jesus' name, Amen.

# Lesson Four: What If I Loved Me Too?

## Day 3

**Key Verses to Memorize:**

Matthew 22:37-39 (NIV) "Jesus replied, 'Love the Lord your God with all your heart and with all your soul and with all your mind.' This is the first and greatest commandment. And the second is like it: "Love your neighbor as yourself.""

Ephesians 2:8 (NIV) "For it is by grace you have been saved, through faith—and this is not from yourselves, it is the gift of God."

**Sister Share Time:**

Grab a cup of coffee and join us for today's **Hey Beautiful Sister Session**– real women, honest conversation. Scan the QR code.

Sister Share Week Four

- Have you recognized any areas you were (or are) being too hard on yourself?
- What helps you receive grace instead of shame?
- What would change in your life if you believed "God's grace is for me too"?

**Mind Shift Moment:**

Old Mind Set: God loves me more when I'm perfect.

New Mind Shift: I am saved by grace, not by perfection.

**Song of the Week:** "Gracefully Broken", by Tasha Cobbs

**Prayer:** Lord God, thank You for being my Teacher. Please Lord keep my heart soft to Your Voice. Lord I want to learn to lean on Your grace and to call on Your power within me to be all that You have purposed me to be. Thank You for never giving up on me. I love You. In Jesus' name, Amen.

# Lesson Four: What If I Loved Me Too?

## Day 4

**Key Verses to Memorize:**

Matthew 22:37-39 (NIV) "Jesus replied, 'Love the Lord your God with all your heart and with all your soul and with all your mind.' This is the first and greatest commandment: And the second is like it: "Love your neighbor as yourself."

Ephesians 2:8 (NIV) "For it is by grace you have been saved, through faith—and this is not from yourselves, it is the gift of God."

**Activity:**

Make mirror truth cards. Take time this week to write one truth about God's love or grace on a card or sticky note and place it on your mirror. Read it every morning. Let God's voice be louder than your inner critic. Need help getting started? Try one of these:

- I am saved by grace through faith, period.
- God's not asking me to be perfect. Just present.
- Grace covers this too
- I am already loved—nothing to prove.

Also, do something kind for yourself

**Mind Shift Moment:**

Old Mind Set: God loves me more when I'm perfect.

New Mind Shift: I am saved by grace, not by perfection.

**Dig Deeper:** Read James 2:14-26

**The Blessing:** May His grace inspire and empower you to live a life that says, "Thank You, God."

**Prayer:** Lord, please forgive me… continue with your own personal prayer.

# Lesson Four: What If I Loved Me Too?

## Day 5

___

**Key Verses to Memorize:**

Matthew 22:37-39 (NIV) "Jesus replied, 'Love the Lord your God with all your heart and with all your soul and with all your mind.' This is the first and greatest commandment. And the second is like it: "Love your neighbor as yourself."

Ephesians 2:8 (NIV) "For it is by grace you have been saved, through faith—and this is not from yourselves, it is the gift of God."

**Declaration Statement:**

I declare_____

**Reflection + Writing Prompts:** "The man who I was- was wrong, but he's the one that built me." Jelly Roll's lyrics from the song, "Unpretty". Have you accepted all of yourself? Imperfect and still worthy of love.

Let this be a transformative moment, a mind-shifting moment, when you see your worth as God sees your worth. What truth is God wanting to write on your heart?

**Mind Shift Moment:**

Old Mind Set: God loves me more when I'm perfect.

New Mind Shift: I am saved by grace, not by perfection.

**The Blessing:** May you offer yourself and others the same grace God does.

**Prayer:** Lord God, I am saved by Jesus' righteousness and not my own. I believe that Your son Jesus Christ's blood on the cross paid for my sin. I believe this, and I receive this amazing grace by faith and faith alone. Lord Jesus, free me from many old laws that I have felt like I had to do to be loved by you. Forgive me for thinking for one moment that my law following earned me salvation when all my offerings are like filthy rags. I deserve hell, but Your grace, and Your love and Your sacrifice bought: freedom for me, freedom from sin, Holy Spirit power within, and a heavenly home one sweet day. I believe You God. In Jesus' name, Amen.

## Lesson Five:

# Taking Down Strongholds – Lies Are No Longer Protected

# Lesson Five: Taking Down Strongholds – Lies Are No Longer Protected
# Day 1

___

**Key Verse to Memorize:**

2 Corinthians 10:4-5 (NIV) "The weapons we fight with are not the weapons of the world. On the contrary, they have divine power to demolish strongholds. We demolish arguments and every pretension that sets itself up against the knowledge of God, and we take captive every thought to make it obedient to Christ."

**Tanya's Story.** Scan the QR code.

Hey Beautiful! Video Lesson Five

**Reflection + Writing Prompts:** Is there a lie I've been protecting in my mind?


Old Mind Set: That's just how I am. I can't help it.

Write your own old mindset or strongholds that God has shown you.

___

New Mind Shift:

I don't protect lies anymore.

I tear down every argument and imagination that sets itself up against the knowledge of God.

I can take every thought captive and make it obedient to Christ.

I am free from _____ (your past stronghold, ex. 'Fear of rejection' or 'I am not enough'.)

**The Blessing:** May you walk in the freedom Jesus has given you today. May you remember that the Word of God is a Sword—powerful, sharp, and ready to fight.

**Prayer:** God, thank You for opening my eyes to the changes I didn't even realize I needed. Thank You for refreshing me. Help me remain committed to the freedom You've shown me. Reveal any areas needing pruning—be gentle with me, Lord. Thank You for loving me tenderly and constantly. In Jesus' name, Amen.

# Lesson Five: Taking Down Strongholds – Lies Are No Longer Protected
# Day 2

**Key Verse to Memorize:**

2 Corinthians 10:4-5 (NIV) "The weapons we fight with are not the weapons of the world. On the contrary, they have divine power to demolish strongholds. 5 We demolish arguments and every pretension that sets itself up against the knowledge of God, and we take captive every thought to make it obedient to Christ."

**Message:**

My stepson was visiting from Ohio. One evening, my husband came home and wanted to spend time with the boys—power washing cars and playing football. I stayed inside for a while, then came out to film them, and later we all watched a movie together.

In the past, the fear of rejection would have crept in: 'Why wasn't I invited outside to play?' or 'I'm not wanted.' But now that the stronghold, fear of rejection, has been demolished, the Holy Spirit helped me take those thoughts captive. The lies were exposed and dealt with. I'm so thankful for the joy and freedom that come from living in Truth.

A stronghold can mean different things depending on how you look at it:

Strongholds can be both good and bad. In Scripture, they're sometimes a refuge- a safe place where God protects and strengthens us, like in 1 Samuel 23:14. But they can also become barriers when they're built around fear, lies, or false security, as seen in 2 Corinthians 10:4. Sometimes the very place that once felt safe can start holding us back, and just like David, God may say, "it's time to come out of the stronghold," so you can step into greater freedom.

Psychologically, it works a lot like confirmation bias. That's when your mind looks for and collects evidence to prove what you already believe—even if it's a lie.

For example, if I believe "I must work to be loved," then every time I do something for someone and they show me love, I store that as proof: 'See? I have to work to be loved.' Over time, this becomes a stronghold—a false belief I protect and live by.

But here's the good news: when we tear down strongholds in Jesus' name, we demolish the walls of the stronghold removing the lies that once held us captive. That's when there's space for God's truth, healing, and peace to take root in our lives.

**Fill in the Blank Section:** 2 Corinthians 10:4-5 (NOV)

The _____ we fight with are not the weapons of the world. On the contrary, they have

_____ power to demolish strongholds. We demolish arguments and every pretension that sets itself up against the _____ of God, and we take captive _____ _____ to make it obedient to _____.

**Reflection + Writing Prompts:** Have I built up a confirmation bias (a wall that is protecting and hiding lies — a stronghold?

**Mind Shift Moment:**

Old Mind Set: That's just how I am. I can't help it.

Write your own old mindset or strongholds that God has shown you.

_____

_____

New Mind Shift:

I don't protect lies anymore.

I tear down every argument and imagination that sets itself up against the knowledge of God.

I can take every thought captive and make it obedient to Christ.

I am free from _____ (your past stronghold, ex. 'Fear of rejection' or 'I am not enough'.)

**Prayer:** Lord God, thank You for purchasing freedom for me! I want to live every day more and more free—free from sin and shame and lies. God, reveal to me lies as soon as the enemy speaks them. And give me Your power to cast them, throw them down. In Jesus' name, Amen

# Lesson Five: Taking Down Strongholds – Lies Are No Longer Protected
# Day 3

**Key Verse to Memorize:**

2 Corinthians 10:4-5 (NIV) "The weapons we fight with are not the weapons of the world. On the contrary, they have divine power to demolish strongholds. 5 We demolish arguments and every pretension that sets itself up against the knowledge of God, and we take captive every thought to make it obedient to Christ."

**Sister Share Time:**

Grab a cup of coffee and join us for today's **Hey Beautiful Sister Session**– real women, honest conversation. Scan the QR code.

Sister Share Week Five

💬What new thing did you learn this week?

💬How have you noticed more freedom in your Spirit?

💬What lies have you identified that you were unable to see before?

**Mind Shift Moment:**

Old Mind Set: That's just how I am. I can't help it.

Write your own old mindset or strongholds that God has shown you.

_____

_____

New Mind Shift:

I don't protect lies anymore.

I tear down every argument and imagination that sets itself up against the knowledge of God.

I can take every thought captive and make it obedient to Christ.

I am free from _____ (your past stronghold, ex. 'Fear of rejection' or 'I am not enough'.)


**Song of the Week:** "Fear is Not My Future", by Brandon Lake + "Break Every Chain" by Tasha Cobbs. "Take it All Back", by Tauren Wells, is one of my favorite songs to declare over my life!!


**Prayer:** Jesus, You said that the Truth would set me free. I believe You. Set me free from… continue with your own personal prayer.

# Lesson Five: Taking Down Strongholds – Lies Are No Longer Protected
# Day 4

**Key Verse to Memorize:**

2 Corinthians 10:4-5 (NIV) "The weapons we fight with are not the weapons of the world. On the contrary, they have divine power to demolish strongholds. 5 We demolish arguments and every pretension that sets itself up against the knowledge of God, and we take captive every thought to make it obedient to Christ."

**Activity:**

Today we're going to create something practical you can carry with you—Truth Cards. These will help you replace lies with God's Word in a way that's simple and powerful.

Grab an index card. On the front, write down a lie that you wrestle with. Write it small—don't give it much space.

Flip the card over. On the back, write a Scripture verse that speaks truth against that lie. This verse will become your weapon whenever the enemy tries to whisper that lie again.

Keep your Truth Card in a place you'll see it often—your Bible, your mirror, your wallet, or even tucked into your phone case.

Each time the lie creeps into your mind, flip the card and say the verse out loud. Over time, you'll not only silence the lie—you'll memorize God's truth and carry it with you wherever you go. As you make more Truth Cards, you can keep them together on a key ring or in a little box as your personal arsenal of God's promises.

**Mind Shift Moment:**

Old Mind Set: That's just how I am. I can't help it.

Write your own old mindset or strongholds that God has shown you.

_____

_____


New Mind Shift:

I don't protect lies anymore.

I tear down every argument and imagination that sets itself up against the knowledge of God.

I can take every thought captive and make it obedient to Christ.

I am free from _____ (your past stronghold, ex. 'Fear of rejection' or 'I am not enough'.)

**The Blessing:** May every lie of the enemy fall powerless, because the strongholds have been torn down In Jesus' name.

**Prayer:** God, as I keep seeking You and learning to walk in this new freedom, remind me throughout the day that my sword—the Word of God—is not just for display but a powerful weapon to fight with. When the enemy tries to convince me that the stronghold still stands, even though I know I have torn it down in Jesus' name, give me the strength to raise my shield of faith and believe You. In Jesus' name, I am free! Amen.

# Lesson Five: Taking Down Strongholds – Lies Are No Longer Protected
# Day 5

---

**Key Verse to Memorize:**

2 Corinthians 10:4-5 (NIV) "The weapons we fight with are not the weapons of the world. On the contrary, they have divine power to demolish strongholds. 5 We demolish arguments and every pretension that sets itself up against the knowledge of God, and we take captive every thought to make it obedient to Christ."

**Declaration Statement:**

I declare_____

**Reflections + Writing Prompts:**

Let this be a transformative moment, a mind-shifting moment, when you see your worth as God sees your worth. What truth is God wanting to write on your heart?

**Mind Shift Moment:**

Old Mind Set: That's just how I am. I can't help it.

Write your own old mindset or strongholds that God has shown you.

_____

_____

New Mind Shift:

I don't protect lies anymore.

I tear down every argument and imagination that sets itself up against the knowledge of God.

I can take every thought captive and make it obedient to Christ.

I am free from _____ (your past stronghold, ex. 'Fear of rejection' or 'I am not enough'.)

**The Blessing:** May you lift your shield of faith and choose to believe God's truth over every thought, feeling, or attack. May you proclaim: "In Jesus' name, I am free—and I will remain free!"

**Prayer:** Lord God, today is a beautiful day. I know that I am walking more confidently as the woman that you have created me to be. Lord, I want to walk in these truths from today into eternity. Grow these roots deep in me. Help me to take the time to feed these truths in the same way that I fed the lies before. Thank you for loving me and being patient with me on this journey. I love you in Jesus' Name. Amen.

# Lesson Six:

# Believing the Truth Over How You Feel

# Lesson Six: Believing the Truth Over How You Feel

## Day 1

**Key Verse to Memorize:**

John 8:31-32 "To the Jews who had believed Him, Jesus said, 'If you hold to my teaching, you are really my disciples. Then you will know the truth, and the truth will set you free.

**Tanya's Story.** Scan the QR code.

Hey Beautiful! Video Lesson Six

**Reflection + Writing Prompts:** What is one lie I used to believe that still tries to show up through emotions? What truth do I know that exposes that lie?

**Mind Shift Moment:**

Old Mind Set: I can't help the way I feel. (So innocent sounding, ugh!)

New Mind Shift:

- Feelings are indicators, not dictators.
- Truth doesn't change, even when emotions do.
- I can feel uncomfortable and still walk in freedom.
- I don't need to obey old patterns - I'm learning to obey truth.
- God's truth holds me together when my emotions feel like they're falling apart.

**The Blessing:** May you walk in the knowing that God's love is immovable and steady.

**Prayer:** Dear Heavenly Father, Thank You for giving me emotions, and thank You even more for giving me truth. I recognize that my feelings are real, but they are not always right. Help me to recognize old emotions when they rise, and to stop and hold them up against Your Word.

Right now, I choose to believe Your truth over how I feel. Even if I feel _____, I know the truth is _____. Wrap me in Your belt of truth. Hold me together when I feel like I'm falling apart. Teach me to pause before I speak, and to walk in the freedom You've already given me. Help me soar above old lies and broken patterns, and to live in the strength that only comes from You. In Jesus' name, Amen.

# Lesson Six: Believing the Truth Over How You Feel

# Day 2

**Key Verse to Memorize:**

John 8:31-32 "To the Jews who had believed Him, Jesus said, 'If you hold to my teaching, you are really my disciples. Then you will know the truth, and the truth will set you free.

**Message:**

This week comes right after our conversation on strongholds for a reason. In my life, the stronghold of fear of rejection had to be torn down in Jesus' name. And once that stronghold came down, the lies inside it were no longer protected. But here's the thing: just because the stronghold is broken doesn't mean I stop feeling old emotions. Sometimes I'll be in a situation, and even though I know it's not rejection, I still feel like it is. That emotional reaction comes from years of seeing things through an old lens. It's uncomfortable, but now I can recognize that those feelings are not the truth, and I have to choose to elevate God's truth above how I feel.

This is where the real work happens. We don't ignore feelings; they're not the enemy. Feelings are indicators. Sometimes they warn us of danger; other times, they are just residues from the past. But the truth is that feelings can ride in the car, but they don't get to drive it. Truth is the driver, not our emotions. Feelings don't get to lead us; truth does.

So, when fear, insecurity, or shame rise, I stop and name it. Then I hold it up against God's truth. One thing that helps me tremendously is speaking truth out loud. Not just thinking it but saying it. Because when I speak it, I hear it, and when I hear it, it strengthens my resolve. For example, I feel rejected, but I know I am chosen. I feel alone, but I know God never leaves me.

You don't need to dig in and rehash every feeling. If God has already exposed the lie, don't camp there. Don't crawl back into the ditch you climbed out of. Don't rehearse the pain but reinforce the truth. Truth is what gathers you back together. It anchors you so you don't unravel.

And don't speak when you're triggered. If you're feeling unseen or undervalued and you know that's tied to an old lie, pause before you call, text, or respond. Delay the reaction. Pray. Speak truth over yourself. Then, if needed, go back and respond from clarity, not from old pain.

That's why Ephesians 6 says the belt of truth holds everything together. "Gird" literally means to wrap it around tightly, so you don't fall apart. And this is where freedom comes in: the truth really does set us free. When we obey truth instead of emotion, we rise above the old lies.

And the view from up there? It's beautiful. Like Isaiah 40:31 promises, when we wait on the Lord, our strength is renewed, and we soar on wings like eagles. That's the freedom Jesus died for. Not that we'd never feel again, but that we'd be free to choose truth even when feelings try to lead.

**Fill-in-the-Blank Section**

John 8:31–32 (NIV)

If you _____ to my _____, you are really my _____. Then you will _____ the _____, and the _____ will set you _____.

**Mind Shift Moment:**

Old Mind Set: I can't help the way I feel. (So innocent sounding, ugh!)

New Mind Shift:

- Feelings are indicators, not dictators.
- Truth doesn't change, even when emotions do.
- I can feel uncomfortable and still walk in freedom.
- I don't need to obey old patterns - I'm learning to obey truth.
- God's truth holds me together when my emotions feel like they're falling apart.

**Reflection + Writing Prompts:** How do I typically react when I feel hurt or rejected? What would it look like to pause and speak truth first?

**Prayer:** Lord God, thank You for setting me free from the strongholds in my life. Please show me when lies are whispering in my ear. God, I believe that I have the power to take captive my thoughts and elevate truth over how I feel. God, continue to feed my faith, and by your power, I will live freer today than I ever have. In Jesus' name, Amen

# Lesson Six: Believing the Truth Over How You Feel

## Day 3

**Key Verse to Memorize:**

John 8:31-32 "To the Jews who had believed Him, Jesus said, 'If you hold to my teaching, you are really my disciples. Then you will know the truth, and the truth will set you free.

**Sister Share Time:**

Grab a cup of coffee and join us for today's **Hey Beautiful Sister Session**— real women, honest conversation. Scan the QR code.

Sister Share Week Six

- When was the last time your feelings told you one thing, but God's Word said another?
- What truth from scripture is hardest for you to hold onto when emotions feel overwhelming?
- Can you think of a time when speaking God's Word out loud shifted how you felt?
- What are some ways you personally delay reacting when emotions rise up?
- How do you remind yourself that emotions are real, but not always reliable?

**Mind Shift Moment:**

Old Mind Set: I can't help the way I feel. (So innocent sounding, ugh!)

New Mind Shift:

- Feelings are indicators, not dictators.
- Truth doesn't change, even when emotions do.
- I can feel uncomfortable and still walk in freedom.
- I don't need to obey old patterns - I'm learning to obey truth.
- God's truth holds me together when my emotions feel like they're falling apart.

**Songs of the Week:** "Speak the Name" by Koryn Hawthorne + "Voice of Truth" by Casting Crowns


**Prayer:** Lord Jesus, I want my mind to be made new. Please forgive me for believing the lie... continue with your personal prayer.

# Lesson Six: Believing the Truth Over How You Feel

# Day 4

**Key Verse to Memorize:**

John 8:31-32 "To the Jews who had believed Him, Jesus said, 'If you hold to my teaching, you are really my disciples. Then you will know the truth, and the truth will set you free.

**Activity:**

Create your Truth Playlist. Create a short playlist of worship songs that remind you of God's truth. The Song of the Week can be the first one.

The next time your emotions feel overwhelming, play one of these songs immediately. While it plays, speak a simple truth statement like:

- "I am loved."
- "God is with me."
- "His Word is greater than my feelings."
- Let music, truth, and worship shift the atmosphere of your heart.

**Mind Shift Moment:**

Old Mind Set: I can't help the way I feel. (So innocent sounding, ugh!)

New Mind Shift:

- Feelings are indicators, not dictators.
- Truth doesn't change, even when emotions do.
- I can feel uncomfortable and still walk in freedom.
- I don't need to obey old patterns - I'm learning to obey truth.
- God's truth holds me together when my emotions feel like they're falling apart.

**The Blessing:** May you know your emotions will follow your thoughts, take them captive.

**Prayer:** God, I am so grateful for the freedom that I'm already experiencing. God, thank you for loving me and being patient with me through my journey. I love You. I worship You. I trust You. In Jesus' name, Amen

# Lesson Six: Believing the Truth Over How You Feel

## Day 5

---

**Key Verse to Memorize:**

John 8:31-32 "To the Jews who had believed Him, Jesus said, 'If you hold to my teaching, you are really my disciples. Then you will know the truth, and the truth will set you free.

**Declaration Statement:**

I declare_____

**Reflections + Writing Prompts:**

Let this be a transformative moment, a mind-shifting moment, when you see your worth as God sees your worth. What truth is God wanting to write on your heart?

**Mind Shift Moment:**

Old Mind Set: I can't help the way I feel. (So innocent sounding, ugh!)

New Mind Shift:

- Feelings are indicators, not dictators.
- Truth doesn't change, even when emotions do.
- I can feel uncomfortable and still walk in freedom.
- I don't need to obey old patterns - I'm learning to obey truth.
- God's truth holds me together when my emotions feel like they're falling apart.

**The Blessing:** May you enjoy the peace of God as you declare Truth over yourself.

    I am worth dying for. God said so.

    I am more than enough, created by the Creator of all.

    I will overcome because nothing is impossible with God.

**Prayer:** Lord God I'm so blessed to know You and experience Your love every day! You are my joy, my peace, my steady! I give myself to You anew today. In Jesus' name, Amen.

# Lesson Seven:

# Sit, Surrender, and Soar

# Week Seven: Sit, Surrender, and Soar

## Day 1

**Key Verse to Memorize:**

Psalm 63:3 (NIV) "Because your love is better than life, my lips will glorify you."

**Tanya's Story.** Scan the QR code.

Hey Beautiful! Video Lesson Seven

**Reflection + Writing Prompts:** Have you ever experienced a "lavender coffee moment"—a small whisper or nudge that led to something beautiful?

**Mind Shift Moment:**

Old Mind Set:

- I have to earn God's love by doing more for Him.
- God is probably disappointed in me because I'm not enough.
- I only feel close to God when I'm perfect or "on fire."
- Resting feels lazy—I should always be serving, working, or proving myself.

New Mind Shift:

- It counts as "Time with God" when I sit in His Presence.
- God's presence isn't earned—it's with me always.
- I will choose to sit, surrender, and soar.
- His love is the safest, most powerful place I can live from.

**The Blessing:** May God's Presence become a normal part of your life.

**Prayer:** My God, my God, my most personal Savior and very best friend. Please remind me to sit in Your presence and soak up Your love every day so that I'm not looking for love from this world but am splashing Your love all over the world. Please help me be attentive to Your voice and learn to be intentional about obeying what You ask in the little moments and the big ones. I ask that You continue to help me sit in Your love. To surrender all of my cares and desires and my whole self to You, and to soar free. In Jesus' name, amen.

# Week Seven: Sit, Surrender, and Soar

## Day 2

---

**Key Verse to Memorize:**

Psalm 63:3 (NIV) "Because your love is better than life, my lips will glorify you."

**Message:**

This final week is all about sitting—not performing, striving, fixing, or asking. Just sitting in the presence of Jesus and letting Him love you whole. This is the full circle of our journey together. We started with love, and we end with it, because love is the root, the fuel, and the destination. Literally, God is Love.

Years ago, while leading a women's Bible study, I came across a book called Practicing the Presence of God by Brother Lawrence. He was a monk whose daily job in the monastery was washing dishes. Yet even at the sink, scrubbing pots and pans, he learned to stay so aware of God's presence that he felt just as close to Him there as in prayer times. That simple book reshaped my days. It showed me that intimacy with God isn't reserved for quiet moments with a Bible open; it can be lived in the middle of chores, conversations, and errands. Learning to really know Him and talk with Him throughout the day is what it means to walk in step with the Spirit.

I now call this my Lavender Coffee Life. Here's why. One day, while driving, the words lavender coffee dropped into my mind. I didn't even know that was a 'real thing'. But I felt nudged to stop at a little coffee shop I was about to pass. They were closed, but the owner happened to be inside. He was grieving the recent loss of one dog, and his other dog was sick. His coffee machine had broken that morning, and he was overwhelmed. As I turned to leave, I spotted a gallon jug of lavender syrup on the counter. Lavender coffee was real—and I knew God had sent me there. I ended up praying with him.

So distracted by God's Presence, I accidentally returned to my office when I wasn't supposed to be there. I was frustrated with myself until I ran into a family that I love, who had been battling addiction. I got to encourage them. That whole day was a Spirit-led rhythm of sitting, listening, and obeying. It reminded me that God's love isn't just poured out when we ask for direction, but it flows freely because He delights in us. And this is where transformation continues: sit in His love. To sit is to pause, rest, and receive. No striving, no proving—just being with Him.

Surrender with hope-filled expectation. Surrender isn't giving up; it's laying down control with the trust that God is good and He is working. It's saying, "I don't have to hold this—You've got me."

Soar with renewed strength. When we've been filled, it's easier to surrender, God lifts us higher. We live lighter, freer, and Spirit-led—like eagles who rise above the chaos on the wind of His presence.

This is the invitation of a Lavender Coffee Life: to sit, surrender, and soar in step with the Spirit—receiving His love, releasing our control, and rising into the life of freedom Jesus already won for us.

**Fill in the Blank Section:** Psalm 63:3 (NIV)

Because your _____ is better than _____, my _____ will _____ you.

**Reflection + Writing Prompts:** How often do you sit in God's presence without needing answers or instructions?

**Mind Shift Moment:**

Old Mind Set:

- I have to earn God's love by doing more for Him.
- God is probably disappointed in me because I'm not enough.
- I only feel close to God when I'm perfect or "on fire."
- Resting feels lazy—I should always be serving, working, or proving myself.

New Mind Shift:

- It counts as "Time with God" when I sit in His Presence.
- God's presence isn't earned—it's with me always.
- I will choose to sit, surrender, and soar.
- His love is the safest, most powerful place I can live from.

**Prayer:** Lord God, thank you for being such a personal God who wants to talk to me. Lord, I'm praying that you begin to show me ways to be aware of Your presence and to pay attention to your voice. I want to get better at responding quickly to the little nudges, as well as the clear directions that you give. Show me yourself this week. Please, Lord, I want to know You more. In Jesus' name, Amen.

# Week Seven: Sit, Surrender, and Soar

## Day 3

---

**Key Verse to Memorize:**

Psalm 63:3 (NIV) "Because your love is better than life, my lips will glorify you."

**Sister Share Time:**

Grab a cup of coffee and join us for today's **Hey Beautiful Sister Session**– real women, honest conversation. Scan the QR code.

Sister Share Week Seven

💬 What is hardest for you: sitting still, surrendering control, or soaring in trust? Why?

💬 Can you describe a time when you felt God's presence in an ordinary moment?

💬 What keeps you from sitting with Jesus?

💬 When you think of "surrender," what do you feel like you're losing? What are you gaining?

**Mind Shift Moment:**

Old Mind Set:

- I have to earn God's love by doing more for Him.
- God is probably disappointed in me because I'm not enough.
- I only feel close to God when I'm perfect or "on fire."
- Resting feels lazy—I should always be serving, working, or proving myself.

New Mind Shift:

- It counts as "Time with God" when I sit in His Presence.
- God's presence isn't earned—it's with me always.
- I will choose to sit, surrender, and soar.
- His love is the safest, most powerful place I can live from.

**Song of the Week:** With You by Elevation Worship


**Prayer:** Lord, I want to stay in Your Presence. Help me ... continue with your own personal prayer.

# Week Seven: Sit, Surrender, and Soar

## Day 4

---

**Key Verse to Memorize:**

Psalm 63:3 (NIV) "Because your love is better than life, my lips will glorify you."


**Activity:**

Practice His Presence. Try one or more of these small, intentional acts to stay aware of God's presence:

- Paint one fingernail a different color as a reminder: Remember God right now
- Put a pokey rock in your pocket to get your attention throughout the day.
- Set a phone alarm that simply says "SIT" or "He loves me."
- Change your screensaver to a phrase like "Surrender + Soar."
- Take a 5-minute pause to do nothing but say, "I'm here, Lord."

These may seem small, but they become anchors for presence awareness. Remember: this is practice, not perfection.


**Mind Shift Moment:**

Old Mind Set:

- I have to earn God's love by doing more for Him.
- God is probably disappointed in me because I'm not enough.
- I only feel close to God when I'm perfect or "on fire."
- Resting feels lazy—I should always be serving, working, or proving myself.

New Mind Shift:

- It counts as "Time with God" when I sit in His Presence.
- God's presence isn't earned—it's with me always.
- I will choose to sit, surrender, and soar.
- His love is the safest, most powerful place I can live from.


**Dig Deeper:** Read John 15:9, Zephaniah 3:17, and 2 Corinthians 3:17


**The Blessing:** May His love pour over you until surrendering feels easy.

**Prayer:** God, thank You for the ways that You are showing me how sweet it is to stay aware of Your Presence all day. Fill me with Your love. I'm ready to live this love ministry all day. In Jesus' name, Amen.

# Week Seven: Sit, Surrender, and Soar

## Day 5

---

**Key Verse to Memorize:**

Psalm 63:3 (NIV) "Because your love is better than life, my lips will glorify you."

**Declaration Statement:**

I declare_____

**Reflections + Writing Prompts:**

Let this be a transformative moment, a mind-shifting moment, when you see your worth as God sees your worth. What truth is God wanting to write on your heart?

**Mind Shift Moment:**

Old Mind Set:

- I have to earn God's love by doing more for Him.
- God is probably disappointed in me because I'm not enough.
- I only feel close to God when I'm perfect or "on fire."
- Resting feels lazy—I should always be serving, working, or proving myself.

New Mind Shift:

- It counts as "Time with God" when I sit in His Presence.
- God's presence isn't earned—it's with me always.
- I will choose to sit, surrender, and soar.
- His love is the safest, most powerful place I can live from.

**The Blessing:** May His love pour over you until surrendering feels easy. (I thought we should say this again).

May you know Him more and more, so much so that you soar in complete confidence in Him.

**Prayer:** Lord, I'm sorry that I go so long without thinking of You. I'm not going to give up, though. I know You're helping me, and I can't wait until being aware of Your presence is like breathing. I love You. In Jesus' name, Amen

# Closing Reflections

Remember, this study is designed to be a beautiful journey, one you can revisit.

As you walked through each page, you were invited into time with the Lord, a sacred space where He gently meets us in our struggles, lifts our gaze, and speaks truth over our hearts. Whether you came with questions, wounds, or simply a desire to draw closer, know this:

**You are deeply, personally, and eternally loved by God.**

This time together doesn't end here. His presence goes with you, and His love continues to speak, day after day, moment by moment.

As you continue growing in God's love, here are some simple ways to keep your heart connected to Him:

- Continue to read and meditate on scripture.
- Begin journaling moments when you see God's love at work in your life.
- Share your testimony of His love with someone who needs encouragement.
- Thank Him daily for His constant presence and affection.

# Contact the Author

♥ Let's Stay Connected

I'd love to hear from you! Whether you're beginning the Hey Beautiful journey, finishing it, or simply looking for encouragement — I'm always grateful to connect.

If you'd like to invite me to speak at a women's event, retreat, or Hey Beautiful gathering, I'd love to come alongside you and share a message of hope and identity in Christ.

You can also reach out for group resources or to order Hey Beautiful shirts.

📧 Email: completelyhis91@gmail.com

📱 Social Media: @Tanya Hall (Facebook)

Let's keep walking in grace and becoming all that God designed us to be. 💕

Completely His,

Tanya Hall

# Memory Verse Cards

**Psalm 63:3**

Because your love is better than life, my lips will glorify you.

**John 8:31-32**

If you hold to my teaching, you are really my disciples. Then you will know the truth, and the truth will set you free.

**Romans 5:8**

But God demonstrates his own love for us in this: While we were still sinners, Christ died for us.

**Ephesians 2:8**

For it is by grace you have been saved, through faith—and this is not from yourselves, it is the gift of God.

**Galatians 6:4**

Each one should test their own actions. Then they can take pride in themselves alone, without comparing themselves to someone else.

**Galatians 1:10**

Am I now trying to win the approval of human beings, or of God? Or am I trying to please people? If I were still trying to please people, I would not be a servant of Christ.

**2 Corinthians 10:4-5**

The weapons we fight with are not the weapons of the world. On the contrary, they have divine power to demolish strongholds. We demolish arguments and every pretension that sets itself up against the knowledge of God, and we take captive every thought to make it obedient to Christ.

www.ingramcontent.com/pod-product-compliance
Lightning Source LLC
Chambersburg PA
CBHW081005180426
43194CB00044B/2827